D0818439

# The NNN

## Triple Net Property Book

## For Buyers of Single Tenant NNN Leased Property

## By Alan Fruitman

President & Managing Broker
Real Estate Foundation, Inc.
Alan@1031tax.com
1.800.454.0015

Printed by CreateSpace

# Acknowledgments

This book is dedicated to my clients, some of whom I have had the privilege of working with since 1993. Clients range from first-time buyers to the largest real estate owners in the United States. Regardless of their experience or net worth, I am humbled and inspired because they have chosen the team at 1031tax.com to help with their real estate investments.

I offer special thanks to my wife Belina, daughter Fiona, and son Rhett. They make coming home every day a priceless treasure.

I give special thanks to my parents, Barbara and Paul, for the family values they instilled in me, education they provided for me, and the copy editing they made within this book.

I especially appreciate Elizabeth Laesecke, Jim Slinkard and Pamela Keith. They are the foundation of 1031tax.com. Their dedication to our clients fosters first-rate properties, communication and satisfaction.

1031tax.com helps investors and 1031 exchange buyers purchase single tenant NNN (and NN) leased property. When I created 1031tax.com, I thought most clients would be participating in a 1031 exchange. To my surprise, each year about half of our property sales are to investors and half are to 1031 exchange buyers.

1031tax.com is our web address and the name by which our company is known. The company's legal name is Real Estate Foundation, Inc. The income properties we sell are the foundation of most of our clients' investments.

My team at 1031tax.com and I hope you enjoy and profit from this book. We encourage you to contact us with ANY comments or questions.

**Alan Fruitman – 1031tax.com**
President & Managing Broker
Real Estate Foundation, Inc.
Alan@1031tax.com
1.800.454.0015

**Properties Closed by Alan Fruitman - 1031tax.com** include various retail and industrial properties, apartment and office buildings. Tenants include 7-Eleven, Aaron's, Advance Auto Parts, Applebee's, Aspen Dental, Alltel, Arby's, AutoZone, Babies R Us, Bank of America, Baskin Robbins, BB&T Bank, Belk, BJ's Wholesale Club, BMO Harris Bank, Buffalo Wild Wings, Burger King, Cato, Chase Bank, Chick-fil-A, Chili's, Cingular Wireless, Cold Stone Creamery, Commerce Bank, CVS Pharmacy, Denny's, Dick's Sporting Goods, Dollar General, Dollar Tree, EB Games, Family Dollar, GameStop, GNC, Great Clips, Gulf Coast MRI, Hallmark, Home Depot, Hooters, H&R Block, Hy-Vee, IHOP, Jackson Hewitt, Jiffy Lube, Joe's Crab Shack, Kash n' Karry, Kay Jewelers, Key Bank, Kirkland's, KFC, KinderCare, Los Angeles Times, McAlister's Deli, McDonald's, Meineke, Napa Auto Parts, NTB, O'Reilly Auto Parts, Outback Steakhouse, Panda Express, Panera Bread, Papa John's Pizza, Payless Shoes, Perkins, Pier 1 Imports, Pizza Hut, PNC Bank, Popeye's, Provident Bank, Regions Bank, Rent-A-Center, Rite Aid, Scottrade, Sofa Express, Sonic, Subway, Starbuck's, Taco Bell, Taco

Cabana, Target, TJ Maxx, United Parcel Service, US Cellular, United States Post Office, Verizon Wireless, Walgreens, Wal-Mart, Wells Fargo Bank, and Wendy's.

Please note that information in this book should not be misconstrued as tax or legal advice. I encourage you to share this information with your CPA and attorney and have them determine if NNN property, 1031 exchange and other topics in this book are appropriate for you.

# Foreword

The NNN Triple Net Property Book, written by real estate broker Alan Fruitman, is a "must" read for anyone interested in investing in income-producing real estate.

This concise work is a step-by-step approach from Letter of Intent to closing, going through what you need to know, what NNN income-producing property is, what an IRC §1031 tax-deferred exchange is, and how to defer taxes on investment real estate, hopefully until you die. After that, your estate should get a stepped-up cost basis and little to no income tax should be paid on the resulting gains.

This is one of the most effective wealth-accumulating strategies available under U.S. federal tax law. As Alan points out in his book, one of the most important aspects of NNN property is the benefit of investing in properties with tenants such as Walgreens, CVS, and McDonalds without the day-to-day hassles of managing investment real estate. This is often a win-

win situation in which the investor minimizes risk, has a strong tenant and, if done correctly, has a prominent location that will appreciate in the long run.

In my 20-plus years as an attorney and CPA representing real estate investors in all aspects of investment real estate and structuring tax-deferred exchanges, Alan Fruitman is one of the most knowledgeable and effective commercial real estate investment advisors I have had the pleasure of working with.

In a world in which most real estate brokers are only after the commission upon sale, Alan brings integrity and honesty by putting his clients' goals and objectives first. He tells it the way it is. If you are looking to invest in NNN property, read this book.

-   Daniel Rosefelt, Attorney & CPA

# Table of Contents

## Chapter 3: About NNN Property

✓ **References Matter**

# Chapter 1:  Why Buy a NNN Property?

## The Phone Rings

The phone rings and a 60-year-old man explains that he wants to "simplify his life".  He has owned and managed an apartment building for 20 years and is tired of tenants who come and go, occasionally pay their rent late, and call with leaky faucets and clogged toilets.  The man has worked hard his entire life and is now ready to travel with his wife and spend time with his children and grandchildren.  The man explains that "managing his apartment building is exhausting and the responsibilities have become increasingly difficult as he gets older."

The man and his wife have close friends who recently sold their apartment building and purchased two single tenant NNN triple net leased properties.  The friends explained that no investment has ever been easier.  Their tenant is required to maintain 100% of the property and pay all taxes and insurance under the NNN lease.  The only time they think about their NNN income property is when the rent check arrives in the mailbox at the beginning of each month.

## Passive vs. Active Income

Passive income is the financial reward for good planning. Passive income from a single tenant NNN property is guaranteed money you receive in your mailbox every month, for 10 to 25 years (often longer), without worrying about vacancy, property management, leaky roofs, clogged toilets, taxes or insurance. Investors purchase NNN property to provide passive income for their family and to fund their retirement. NNN property also will be an anchor in the financial legacy you leave when you pass.

The opposite of passive income is active income. Active income is money you receive from your day job or "hands-on" investments such as apartment buildings, office buildings and shopping centers. It takes a significant amount of time and energy to produce active income.

# NNN Properties Are Not for Everyone

Some people like to micromanage their investments and enjoy dealing with the day-to-day projects. Some apartment building or shopping center owners like to fix things and show prospective tenants vacant units. They like to occupy their time with active management. People of this nature would be bored if they owned a NNN property.

Property with a true NNN lease (also known as a "bond lease" or "absolute net lease") is best suited for the investor who wants no property management responsibilities. When you own a NNN property, your tenant will maintain and pay for 100% of the physical property, common area maintenance, taxes and insurance.

# Baby Boomers, Retirees, Doctors, Attorneys & Other Professionals

Baby Boomers, retirees and many other professional people own a tremendous amount of real estate (apartment buildings, office buildings, shopping centers, etc.). They have worked for decades, built considerable wealth and know that it takes significant attention to detail to actively manage and properly maintain their investment property. They also know active management and property maintenance will become increasingly difficult as they get older. When Baby Boomers retire, they want to travel and enjoy time with their family. Baby Boomers know that leaving an apartment building or shopping center to their spouse or children could pose a daunting burden when they pass.

## Three Investment Goals

Baby Boomers, retirees, doctors, attorneys and many other professionals have three main goals for their investments. Goal #1 is passive income (eliminate active management). Goal #2 is preservation of equity. Goal #3 is appreciation of value.

These goals are often achieved when you own a NNN property, especially when you invest for the long-term.

## Strong Guarantee & Prominent Location

Property owners sleep well at night when their tenant is financially strong. This is why a strong tenant is often the first item on an investor's criteria list. Fortunately, many NNN properties are leased by companies that are considered "Investment Grade" by Standard & Poors. These companies often have a multi-billion-dollar market capitalization. Examples include Walgreens, CVS, Starbucks, McDonald's, Chipotle, Chase Bank, Wells Fargo, AutoZone, Home Depot, Dollar General, Target, and other brand name retail tenants. (Market capitalization is the value of a publicly traded company. Value equals the total shares times the current market price of each share.)

Is it possible that one of these investment grade tenants will become bankrupt and therefore not be able to fulfill the lease obligations? Yes. Is it likely? No.

Having a strong tenant is certainly important. However, a prominent location should be an investor's most important criterion. Here's why: Over time, a property with a prominent location and average tenant will trump a property with an average location and a great tenant. Fortunately, NNN properties are usually located in prominent locations.

Have you ever seen a Walgreens, McDonald's or Chase Bank in a location that you would not be proud to own? Have you ever seen a vacant CVS, AutoZone or McDonald's? The answer to these questions is probably "no".

## Own a Piece of the Rock

Have you ever wondered which of your assets have permanent value? Do you realize that many assets can have significant value one day and no value the next day? A tangible or hard asset such as real estate, a gold watch or diamond ring has permanent value. A paper asset such as a stock, bond or your tenant's lease may not.

If you own a stock or bond from one of the companies referenced above, or from any other company, you own a piece of paper with a promise of repayment or income.

In essence, you have a dual guarantee when you own NNN property. You will own both a paper asset and a tangible asset. The paper asset is a lease with a promise to pay; the tangible asset is real estate.

## Chapter 2: What NNN Buyers Need To Know

## Relationships Mean More Than Money

You could be a world-class singer but you may never sell a single record. You could have the cure for cancer but you may never save a single life. You could be a qualified candidate but you may not get hired. You could submit a full-price offer to purchase a NNN property but the seller may not accept your offer. Being a good person, ready, willing and financially able may not be enough in the ultra-competitive process of securing the right NNN property.

Quick story – One of my investors submitted a full-price offer to purchase a Chase Bank. The seller received more than twenty offers the first day the property came to market. Eleven of the offers were full-price or above full-price. The seller's broker and I had closed many properties in the past. The broker called me and asked how well I knew my buyer and if I could vouch for his financial ability and his personal credibility. I assured the broker that my buyer would close the transaction (upon completion of satisfactory due diligence) if the seller accepted his offer. To make a long story short, the seller did not initiate a bidding war nor did he accept the above-full-price offers. The seller accepted my client's full-price offer based on my personal assurances.

In the transaction above, the seller turned down more than twenty written offers. Even though many of the buyers were ready, willing and financially able, only one buyer had a broker with the right credibility and relationship.

**Buy and Hold**

Although some investors purchase a NNN property and sell it for a quick profit, most NNN property investors hold their property for many decades.

Think like Warren Buffet, who is famous for buying stock in a quality company and almost never selling it. He is not focused on how the value changes from year to year. Mr. Buffet is confident that a quality company will prosper and continue to prosper.

The same long-term principle is true – along with the additional security from the underlying real estate – for NNN property. If you purchase a NNN property with a quality tenant and location, it is very likely that your tenant will fulfill all lease obligations. In addition, when your tenant eventually vacates, the quality property you purchased many years earlier should be significantly more valuable (assuming market rents have risen).

**Location Matters**

Location matters when you purchase a NNN property. Strong demographics and a prominent parcel are the keys to long-term success. The property should have more than enough nearby residents who need the product or service that your tenant provides. The property should have strong visibility from the main road and easy access for clients to enter and leave. In addition, a location close to many other tenants has the advantage of being a destination for shoppers. For example, a strong retail property would be located on a prominent street with surrounding tenants such as Chase Bank, Wells Fargo, Walgreens, CVS, Wal-Mart, Home Depot, Lowe's, McDonald's, Chipotle, O'Reilly, AutoZone, 7-Eleven, etc.

Quick story – One of my clients is an appraiser who understands the importance of real estate fundamentals. He purchased an Advance Auto Parts building many states away from where he lived. The property was in a low income area but there were more than 500,000 residents within a five-mile radius. The client knew that the surrounding residents were likely to fix their cars rather than get a new car every few years. In addition, when the lease for Advance Auto Parts eventually ends, there should be significant need for other retailers to service such a large amount of people.

## Long-Term Leases Are All About Control

Tenants are willing to sign a long-term NNN lease because they want to control the property. Tenants spend considerable money when they fixture and brand the property they rent. Tenants often remodel their store in order for the property to look fresh, modern and inviting. A tenant's worst fear is for the landlord to not extend their lease when the primary term and renewal options expire.

Landlords like long-term NNN leases because they want control over their long-term investments. Control means you have a steady income stream and no vacancy, leasing commissions or other expenditures.

## Locations Become Branded

A company's brand is more than just the product it sells. A company's brand is also its location. For example, you know exactly how far the closest Starbuck's, Chase Bank and Walgreens are to your home. These companies have branded their locations in your mind. When you crave hot coffee or tea, need cash or want to pick up a prescription from the pharmacy, you know where to go. Consumers are creatures of habit who like consistency.

Companies become successful when they fulfill the needs and expectations of their customers. Therefore, companies pick prominent locations, meticulously maintain the property and often stay in the same place as long as they can. This includes the primary lease term and option periods, even longer if possible.

**Two Happiest Days of Owning a NNN Property**

The two happiest days of owning a NNN property are the day you purchase your property and the day your tenant's lease expires. Here's why: When you purchase a NNN property with a creditworthy tenant, it is extremely likely that your tenant will fulfill its obligations throughout the primary lease term. This means you will receive a rent check, every month, for 10-25 years. In addition, tenants often extend their lease throughout the option periods. This means you could receive uninterrupted cash flow for 30, 40, 50 or more years.

The second happiest day of NNN property ownership is the day the final option period of your tenant's lease expires. Here's why: Your property gets a "second lease on life" when the tenant's lease expires. This means you can negotiate a brand new lease with your current tenant or you can rent your property to an entirely new tenant. Either way, the new lease will be at the new market rental rate.

Think back 20 or 30 years. Rents were very low relative to today. Now imagine how high rents might be 20 or 30 years in the future. Again, the two happiest days of owning a NNN property are the day you purchase your property and the day your tenant's lease expires.

## Low Cap Is Safe…High Cap Is Dangerous

In baseball terms, owning NNN property with a low cap rate is similar to hitting a single or double. Owning NNN property with a high cap rate is similar to swinging hard and hoping for a home run.

Cap rate is the rate of return on your investment. For example, if you purchase a $1,000,000 NNN property with a 6% cap rate, your annual net operating income will be $60,000.

There is usually a direct correlation between cap rate and risk. Creditworthy tenants, prominent locations and long leases are the low-risk attributes most NNN investors seek. Naturally, these low-risk attributes yield a lower rate of return than properties that have inferior tenants, average locations or shorter leases.

Remember, most NNN property owners are Baby Boomers, retirees, doctors, attorneys, CPAs and other professionals with safety and passive income as their primary objectives. Hitting a single or double is not sexy, but it's safe. Hitting a home run sounds like fun, but you are much more likely to strike out.

If a high cap rate is your priority, ask yourself: "How much risk am I willing to take?"

**Is It Okay to Pay Full-Price?**

You probably purchased your first home many years ago for significantly less money than it is worth today. You were a young professional who knew that buying a home would be a financial and personal foundation for all of life's experiences yet to come. You called a real estate agent and asked him or her which neighborhoods were safe and would be a sound investment. You were cautious because it was probably your largest investment at that stage of your life. Hopefully you knew that picking the right property, a property in a quality neighborhood that you would enjoy coming home to every day, was more important than getting a few thousand dollars off the price.

Fast forward to today. You have tremendous life experience and have most likely purchased additional properties. You successfully negotiated the price of some properties and paid full-price for others. Regardless of the potential negotiation, any property you purchased in the past is most likely worth much more today than when you purchased it.

Since you are reading this book, it is safe to assume that you are interested in purchasing a NNN property. Let's assume you are ready now, the NNN market is hot (it almost always is) and you just found a property that is priced competitively and fits your specific criteria. The price is $3,000,000, the location is prime, and similar properties in less desirable areas are under contract. How should you proceed?

Understanding the market and your competition is very important. Demand for NNN properties is usually very high. When a NNN property with a strong tenant, long-term lease and quality location comes to market, the seller often receives multiple full-price offers the first day on the market. Therefore, if you submit an offer for less than full-price and the seller receives multiple full-price offers, the seller will not consider or counter your offer. The seller will choose among the full-price offers. However, if there are other properties on the market that have attributes similar to the one you are considering, submitting an offer for less than full-price could be a smart decision.

Please remember that buying the "right property" is more important than saving a few dollars.

## Build a Diversified Portfolio

You know that "location, location, location" is the key to successful real estate investment. Hopefully you also know that "diversification, diversification, diversification" is the key to success in your overall portfolio.

Buying a home was probably your first large investment. As you accumulated additional money, you had to figure out where to invest next. You probably purchased stocks or additional property.

# Diversification

Over time, as your investments appreciated and your overall net worth grew, hopefully you didn't keep all of your money in one stock or one investment property. If you believe in stocks, hopefully you built a diversified stock portfolio. If you believe in real estate, hopefully you built a diversified real estate portfolio.

Building a diversified portfolio of NNN property is relatively easy because ownership is not a burden. Your tenant maintains 100% of the property and pays 100% of the taxes and insurance. Diversification in NNN properties could include location, type of tenant and duration of lease. For example, you could own property leased to a bank (Wells Fargo or Chase), a pharmacy (Walgreens or CVS), a restaurant (McDonald's or Starbucks) or an auto parts store (AutoZone or O'Reilly). The properties could be located in several quality cities and the lease durations could be staggered among 10, 15, 20 or 25 years (plus renewal options).

For example, if you own an apartment building or shopping center worth $5,000,000 you can sell your property, utilize a 1031 tax deferred exchange (defined later in this book) and purchase two or three NNN properties. This diversification will mean you are not dependent on the economic conditions of one city, one industry or year-to-year changes in the economy.

## High Leverage = Risk

Most people with significant wealth were risk takers at some point in their life. Buying real estate with high leverage is how great fortunes are made (and lost). The greater the leverage, the greater the potential reward. Coincidentally, most real estate brokers tell their clients that high leverage is good; the more properties a client buys, the larger the commission for the broker.

Unfortunately, along with potential reward comes potential risk. One of the risky aspects of high leverage is that investment property loans often have a balloon payment. This means that after a certain

*Do not over-leverage — pay cash for at least 50% of purchase price.*

number of years, you will be required to refinance or pay off your loan. If property values increase and interest rates remain low, it should be easy to refinance and your high-leverage investment will be financially rewarded. If property values decrease or interest rates rise, you could have a difficult time refinancing and high leverage will be financially painful.

There comes a time in most people's life when preserving their assets becomes more important than trying to exponentially increase them. This transition normally comes around the time of retirement. When you retire, safe and predictable income is normally the top priority.

NNN properties are considered a conservative investment. This means NNN property buyers are generally conservative investors. Many NNN buyers avoid leverage altogether and pay cash for their property. When financing a NNN purchase, most buyers do not over-leverage. If you leverage 75%, you may be in the danger zone. If you leverage 50% or lower, you most likely will be safe.

## Which States Should You Target or Avoid?

One of the biggest mistakes NNN buyers make is to only look for property close to where they live. This desire is understandable because owning property close to home is comfortable. Although buying a local property can be achieved, you will likely have few properties to choose from.

If you live in Manhattan, Miami or Los Angeles, the selection of available NNN properties will be slim and the capitalization rate (rate of return) will be very low. You will have many more choices if you are open to properties in or near quality cities such as Houston, Dallas, Atlanta, Chicago, Scottsdale, Denver, Seattle or Portland.

It is natural for you to favor certain states. However, it would be a mistake to completely eliminate other states from your consideration. Every state has prominent retail locations where your tenant and your property will prosper. If you are a resident of an income-tax-free state (Florida, Texas, Tennessee,

Nevada, Washington, South Dakota, Alaska, New Hampshire or Wyoming), there is definitely a financial advantage if you purchase a property in your state or one of the other income-tax-free states.

The goal of most NNN property buyers is to have a financially solid tenant who will occupy the property for the next 20, 30 or 40+ years. Buyers also want to ensure that their property will be easy to re-tenant when their current tenant eventually vacates. The recipe for achieving these goals revolves around the following property characteristics: prominent location, synergy with many other national tenants, strong visibility from heavily trafficked roadway, and an established and growing demographic. If you focus on a location where your tenant will prosper, rather than on a particular state, your investment property should prosper for generations.

When marketing a NNN property, most developers or listing real estate brokers put together a comprehensive property brochure that details all lease terms. The brochure will often have an aerial photo of the property and surrounding areas as well as a demographic report. In addition to the brochure, you are able to view almost any address and street using Google Street View ®. For fun, do a Google search of your home, work or any other address. Click "Street View" and navigate with your mouse up and down the street. The visual will be as if you are driving down the street in your car. You get a great understanding of most properties by viewing the property address in Street View.

## Why Lowball Offers Don't Work

Everyone loves a deal, but you must be careful what you ask for. The marketplace for NNN property is almost always hot and demand is usually much stronger than supply.

If a property is priced **below** market value, the seller will receive countless offers, many of which will be above full-price. If a property is priced **at** market value, the seller will receive many offers, most of which will be at or within a slight variance from full-

*Be careful when making low-ball offers.*

price. If a property is priced **above** market value, the seller will receive offers that reflect the realistic market price. In each scenario, the seller also will receive lowball offers but these offers will be ignored. The common theme is that there is generally not a shortage of offers and market value will be evident to the seller.

If you like the property and you submit a lowball offer, you will lose credibility. <u>The seller will think you are looking for a deal and you will be difficult to work with.</u> The seller may not consider your revised offer because your credibility will be lost.

## What Does Your Real Estate Broker Do?

Every football team has a quarterback. Some quarterbacks win the Super Bowl and add great value to their team; others retire with a losing record. Think of your NNN property broker as the quarterback for your transaction.

Here's why your NNN property broker must be a Most Valuable Player:

Finding properties on the Internet is easy. Showing you pre-market or off-market NNN properties may be the difference between your buying an average property or a trophy property.

Confirming that a property is still available is easy. Asking the seller or seller's broker preliminary questions and identifying potential environmental, boundary or other problems before submitting a Letter of Intent will save you time and money.

Writing a Letter of Intent is easy. Crafting a Letter of Intent that will pass your test, the test of your attorney, the seller's broker, the seller's attorney and the seller is a balancing act and a true art form.

Having the seller accept a Letter of Intent is easy if there are no other offers. Having the seller accept your Letter of Intent when there are multiple equivalent offers is the difference between your securing the right property or having the right property slip away.

*A wise man knows everything;*
*A shrewd man knows everybody.*

Contract negotiations are easy when your attorney and the seller's attorney get along and agree on terms. Sharing insight and communicating with you, your attorney and the seller's broker is critical when your attorney and the seller's attorney are at an impasse.

Understanding and coordinating the earnest money deposit, due diligence, contract deadlines and closing are easy if you are an experienced NNN property buyer and your attorney diligently monitors your transaction. Making sure your contract deadlines are not missed, working through issues, recognizing which issues should not be accepted, sharing insight from prior transactions and being available for your questions are the sound contributions a skilled NNN broker can provide.

## It's Whom Your Broker Knows

There is an old proverb that says, "A wise man knows everything; a shrewd one, everybody." This proverb should make you think. The proverb applies to most things in life, including real estate. If your real estate broker knows everything but not everybody, he or she will have answers to all of your questions. However, he or she will lack relationships, pre-market and off-market properties.

NNN property is a tiny niche within the aggregate real estate market. Within this niche, there is a small network of real estate brokers across the United States that sells the majority of these properties. The brokers all know each other. They know which brokers are trustworthy, properly educate their clients, don't disappear when the contract is signed, have the acumen to work through problems, and won't circumvent their client relationships. If your broker is a trusted insider within the NNN property community, you will have access to many properties before they come to market. If you do not have access to an insider's connections, you will only see properties posted on the Internet.

## Whom Does Your Broker Represent?

When a SELLER is represented by a real estate broker, the broker has a fiduciary responsibility to provide accurate advice, information and every possible legal advantage to the seller. When the seller's broker markets the seller's property, the broker's only goal is to convince a buyer to purchase that property. If the seller's broker doesn't convince a buyer to purchase this specific property, he or she does not get paid. Once again, a seller's broker's job is to convince a buyer to purchase the seller's specific property.

When a BUYER is represented by a real estate broker, the broker has a fiduciary responsibility to provide accurate advice, information and every possible legal advantage to the buyer. The buyer's broker must provide the buyer with many quality properties to choose from. Since commissions are relatively standard, the buyer's broker does not have a financial incentive to sell one property versus another. The buyer broker's job is to make sure the client reviews many properties and chooses the one that best fits the client's investment criteria. The buyer's broker knows that if he or she provides exceptional service and advice to the client, the client will purchase future properties and refer friends and business associates.

## How the Seller Views You

A seller choosing the right buyer is similar to betting on the right horse. When betting on a horse race, there are many horses to choose from. When selling a quality NNN property, there are many buyers to choose from. When betting on a horse, you only get paid if your horse finishes in the money. When selling a property, the seller only gets paid if the buyer closes. Therefore, it is a waste of time and money if the wrong horse or the wrong buyer is chosen. A seller wants to make sure the buyer does not tie up the property for several weeks or months without closing.

Presentation is everything when your buyer broker submits a Letter of Intent to the seller. Presentation is the difference between looking like the author of an anonymous piece of paper and looking like a conscientious purchaser with the integrity, financial ability and character to close the property. Once the seller understands your story, your enthusiasm for the property and your financial ability, the seller is much more likely to accept your offer.

Your real estate broker not only represents you; your broker is the representation of you. Your broker is your advocate, your voice and the face of your transaction. The credentials and confidence a broker conveys often will determine which full-price offer the seller chooses.

**A Seller Wants Three Things**

Price, contingency period and closing date are the three hot-button items for a seller.

A seller's top priority is usually price. This point is self-explanatory. Next, a seller wants a short contingency period. The shorter the contingency period, the sooner the buyer's analysis of the property is complete and the earnest money deposit becomes non-refundable. Last but not least, the closing date is very important. Some sellers want to close quickly so they can receive their money and move on. Other sellers want a delayed closing date so they have time to find a replacement property.

## Your Attorney Can Help or Hurt You

Most NNN real estate transactions have two attorneys; one attorney represents the seller and one represents the buyer. Both attorneys must be diligent when they review the purchase contract, lease, title commitment, loan documents (if applicable), due diligence materials and closing documents. At the same time, they must be careful not to be overbearing and one-sided. If your attorney is both diligent and reasonable, your transaction will most likely end with a successful closing. If your attorney battles over every item, your transaction will be destined for stalemate.

It is always advisable to have an experienced real estate attorney represent you when buying or selling a NNN property. Just make sure your attorney does not nitpick at the contract and only fights the important battles.

## Is an Environmental Problem a Deal Breaker?

Would you purchase a used car without having a mechanic check it out? Clearly the answer to this question is "no". The same rings true when you buy a NNN property. Even if the property is new construction, the land isn't new. A relatively inexpensive environmental study is money well spent.

The industry standard and preliminary investigation is a Phase 1 Environmental Site Assessment (ESA). The Phase 1 provider will visit the property and look for above-ground oil tanks, spills or other visible items of concern. The provider will research the prior uses of the property and surrounding properties, and review public records for water or soil contamination, hazardous substances, petroleum products and underground storage tanks. In addition, a vapor test is often used to detect contaminants.

If the Phase 1 ESA identifies potential concern, a Phase 2 ESA can be performed. Phase 2 ESA is a soil, groundwater and surface water test. When conducting a Phase 2 ESA, samples are collected by drilling holes into various parts of the parcel. The soil and water are tested for chemicals and other contaminants.

Environmental problems can linger and be very expensive to resolve. If you are not an expert in environmental problems, you should be very cautious if one is identified.

## Chapter 3:  About NNN Property

### Pros and Cons of a Ground Leased Property

Let's start with the definition of a ground lease.
Ground lease is a form of ownership in which you own
the land and your tenant constructs, owns and pays for
the building.  When your tenant finally vacates, you
inherit the residual building (see lease for specific
details).  Some people only purchase ground leases.
Other people would never own a ground lease.
Ground leases make up approximately 20% of all
NNN properties.

Here are three advantages of owning a ground lease:

#1 - Since your tenant constructed and paid for the
building, the rent is based on an enhanced land value
(enhanced because there is a long-term lease to a high
credit tenant).  Therefore, rent is usually much lower
than it would be if the tenant did not pay to construct
the building.

#2 - Your tenant spent considerable time and money constructing the property and is very likely to occupy it as long as possible.

#3 – You usually walk into immediate equity because your tenant built and paid for the building. You are happy if the tenant stays (uninterrupted cash flow) and if the tenant vacates (upside in rent).

Here are two disadvantages of owning a ground lease:

#1 – The capitalization rate (rate of return) is lower than a fee simple property because you usually walk into immediate equity / upside.

#2 – Because you don't own the building, there is nothing to depreciate.

## Pros and Cons of a Fee Simple Property

Fee simple is the traditional form of ownership in which you own the land and the building. This is how most real estate is owned. Fee simple makes up approximately 80% of all NNN properties.

One advantage of owning fee simple property is the relatively higher cap rate (compared to a ground lease). In addition, you are able to depreciate the physical building. Depreciation is used to offset rental income.

The main disadvantage of owning a fee simple property is it costs more money to purchase than a ground lease. The property is more expensive because you are buying the land and the building.

## Why Most People Avoid Leasehold Property

Leasehold, also known as land lease, is not ownership; it is the right to use a property for a predetermined number of years. When the leasehold term expires, all rights revert to the property owner. Leasehold has no residual value when the term expires.

Leasehold makes up less than 1% of NNN properties. It is only being discussed because many people mistakenly interchange the term ground lease with leasehold.

## Lease Terms are Permanent...Unless They Are Changed

The lease between landlord and tenant will meticulously outline all of the rights and obligations for each party. The lease terms are permanent unless the landlord and tenant mutually agree to a lease amendment. When a change is desired, it is usually initiated by one of the parties. This is when a proverbial game of poker begins. If one party has a need, the other can take advantage of it. However, be careful to not overplay your hand.

The most common lease amendment revolves around an extension of term and a higher or lower rent. For example, the tenant often becomes concerned when the lease only has a few years remaining. The tenant, not wanting to be at the mercy of the landlord, will initiate an extension of term. The landlord can choose to negotiate or let the lease expire. On the flip side, the landlord may propose a change when the lease becomes short and a vacancy could occur.

**Are You Sitting on Cash?**

There's a saying about money: You are financially comfortable when you have enough spending money to not worry about day-to-day expenses. You are wealthy when all of your spending money comes from the income of your investments.

Are you sitting on cash? How much income is your cash generating? Converting your cash into an income property should yield a significant financial benefit compared to your waiting one year, two years, three years or longer to invest.

If you are committed to purchasing a NNN property, make sure you work with a real estate broker who specializes in NNN property. Buying a NNN property through the broker who sold you an apartment or office building often will hurt you more than help you. Make sure your NNN broker has established relationships with other NNN owners, developers and real estate brokers; shows you many tenants and properties across the country; compares and contrasts the tenants and locations; dedicates time to answer all of your questions; can identify a pitfall before it appears, and has the experience to guide you through an easy or complicated purchase.

## Who Owns the Properties for Sale?

You see NNN properties such as Walgreens, Burger King, Wells Fargo, Starbuck's, Advance Auto Parts and Home Depot when you drive around town. Most people do not know that these properties are owned by people like you – not by the companies themselves.

Walgreens is in the business of selling pharmaceuticals and other goods; Burger King is in the business of selling burgers and fries. If Walgreens or Burger King allocated their money to owning property, they would have less available money to expand their business. This is why most national tenants do not own their real estate.

National companies have an in-house real estate department that identifies strategic locations for expansion. Demographics, traffic counts and proximity to other national retailers are a few of the metrics used to pinpoint new locations. The real estate department works with one of its preferred developers to construct a "build-to-suit" property based on a specific architectural plan.

The developer signs a lease with the tenant, purchases the land and constructs the building. The developer knows there is significant demand from the investment community to purchase the property once construction is complete, a Certificate of Occupancy is received, rent commences and the tenant opens for business.

*Landlord should have no maintenance obligations.*

Some developers keep the property as a long-term investment; most sell the property and move to their next project.

## Not All NN or NNN Leases Are the Same

NNN means triple net, nothing else. NNN lease is a hot buzzword and listing brokers frequently market their listings as NNN, even when they are really NN (double net). If you see a brochure that states the lease is NNN, with the landlord having any maintenance obligations, you should recognize the lease is really NN.

There is considerable variation between one NN lease and another. Some NN leases are relatively landlord friendly with the only obligation being structure. Other NN leases have roof, structure, HVAC, parking lot and other maintenance obligations.

There is commonality between each tenant and its respective lease structures. An experienced NNN real estate broker can quickly recognize when information is inaccurate or misleading. Access to this insight will save you a tremendous amount of time and money. In addition to guidance from your broker, it is important that you and your attorney carefully review the lease and understand all rights and obligations.

## Tenants Prefer Free-Standing Property

When a fashion model walks down the runway, he or she walks alone. When walking alone, the model stands out and all attributes are seen. The same is true for a free-standing NNN property. A free-standing property is located in front of an anchored retail center or adjacent to the main thoroughfare. The property usually will have distinguished and individualized signage, easy ingress and egress, drive-thru access and designated parking.

The opposite of a free-standing retail property is "in-line." If you are a tenant in an in-line shopping center, you are squeezed between other tenants. In-line tenants are located further from the main thoroughfare and have limited signage and shared parking. In-line retail space is usually in less demand and commands a lower rent per foot than free-standing property.

## Big Box vs. Smaller Box

A big box property such as Home Depot or Wal-Mart often contains more than 100,000 square feet. A smaller box property such as CVS, Taco Bell, Chase Bank, Dollar General, Chipotle or O'Reilly Auto Parts usually has between 2,000 and 15,000 square feet.

There are countless uses for a smaller box when the tenant vacates. If CVS vacates a 15,000 square foot property, one tenant can fill the space or it is relatively easy to partition the building into several spaces. If Wal-Mart vacates a 100,000 square foot space, it may be difficult to find one replacement tenant. You can partition the space but you still will need to find several significant replacement tenants.

It is important to remember that real estate is permanent, tenants are temporary. Here are a few multi-million-dollar questions you should ask yourself:

What will happen when my tenant vacates? How easy will it be for me to find a new tenant? How much work will I have to do to make my vacant property marketable? If my tenant has 15 years remaining on its primary lease term, how much rent do I anticipate my property will command 15 years from now (in case my tenant does not exercise its renewal option)?

## Does Your Property Need to Be Close to Where You Live?

An apartment building, office building or shopping center should be located close to where you live. These properties require intense property management. Tenants constantly turn over, repairs are needed and income is lost every day from when your tenant vacates to when your new tenant begins paying rent. You also have to pay leasing commissions. If you hire a property manager, it is prudent for you to manage the manager.

Owning a NNN leased property will be a completely different experience. Because your tenant maintains and pays for 100% of repairs, there is no benefit for the property to be located close to where you live. The most important thing is to select a property in an established, stable and growing location.

## Franchise vs. Corporate Lease

Most leases from the following companies are guaranteed by the parent corporation (corporate lease): Walgreens, CVS, Home Depot, Lowe's, Target, Wal-Mart, Kohl's, Starbuck's, Chick-fil-A, McDonald's, Chipotle, AutoZone, O'Reilly Auto Parts, Advance Auto Parts, Dollar General, Family Dollar, Dollar Tree, FedEx, Wawa, 7-Eleven, Sheetz, Dick's Sporting Goods, Mattress Firm, Chase Bank, Wells Fargo, Bank of America, PNC Bank, BB&T Bank, TD Bank, Fresenius, DaVita, Aspen Dental, Tractor Supply, Sprouts and Whole Foods.

Many leases from the following companies are guaranteed by the franchisee: Arby's, Burger King, AT&T, Verizon, Pizza Hut, Long John Silver's, KFC, Taco Bell, Dunkin Donuts, Panera Bread, Golden

Corral, Jiffy Lube, Buffalo Wild Wings, Wendy's, IHOP, Applebee's, Hardee's, Dairy Queen, Hooters, Jack in the Box, Sonic, Denny's, Aaron's Rents, Goodwill and Carl's Jr.

Some franchisees are very strong and have hundreds of locations under their franchise umbrella. Other franchisees are small, with as few as one location, but are financially stable.

A combination of the tenant's credit and the property's location must be considered before you draw a conclusion whether to buy a corporate-guaranteed or franchise-guaranteed property. Remember, over time, a property with a prominent location and average tenant will trump a property with an average location and a great tenant. If a franchisee happens to go bankrupt because of mismanagement or overall poor performance and your specific property is still prosperous, it is common for the parent company or another franchisee to take over operations and fulfill the existing lease.

## Chapter 4: From The Beginning

## Heed These Nine Warnings

Buying a NNN property is similar to picking a spouse. It is painful and costly if you make a mistake.

# 1 – Select a real estate broker who specializes in NNN property. If your broker offers to help you purchase an apartment or office building, you are working with the wrong broker.

# 2 – Ask your broker specific questions. If your broker needs to research each answer, you are working with the wrong broker.

# 3 – Verify references. If your broker does not have a long list of satisfied clients, you are working with the wrong broker.

# 4 – Require opinions. If your broker does not guide you and help you understand the difference between

various tenants, lease structures and locations, you are working with the wrong broker.

# 5 – Make sure your broker represents you. If your broker represents the seller, you are working with the wrong broker.

#6 – Don't sign an exclusive agreement. If your broker wants you to sign an exclusive buyer agreement, you are working with the wrong broker.

# 7 – Review many properties. If your broker does not constantly show you new NNN properties, you are working with the wrong broker.

# 8 – Don't rely on the Internet. If your broker does not send you "Pre-Market" or "Off-Market" properties, you are working with the wrong broker.

# 9 – Accept only the best service. If your broker does not take the time to answer all of your questions and return all of your calls in a timely manner, you are working with the wrong broker.

## May You Call Me Five Times a Day?

Remember when your kindergarten teacher said, "There are no dumb questions." The same rule applies when you buy a NNN property. You are an expert at something (perhaps medicine or law). Your broker must be an expert in NNN properties.

Your broker should make you feel as if you are the most important client. You absolutely may call your broker five times a day. When you speak with your broker frequently, you not only gain insight and information; you also develop synergy. Your broker will learn how you think, what is important to you, and what your short-term and long-term goals are. This insight will enable your broker to make recommendations based on *your* goals, not his or her personal bias.

## Be a Decision Maker

Buying NNN property is different than buying any other type of real estate. The credit rating and lease structure will vary among tenants. The demographic and quality of location will vary among properties. You should "window shop" before buying – review many property brochures and ask your NNN real estate broker many questions.

Once you understand the NNN property market and have confidence in your broker, it is time to get serious. You must be serious because you will have a lot of competition. There is always a long line of well-qualified buyers who will jump on a quality NNN property the first day it comes to market. When your broker sends you the right property, you must be a decision maker.

## The Process & the Property

There are two distinct components of buying NNN property – the process and the property. Understanding only one is like driving a car with a gas pedal, but no brake. You're destined to be out of control and, most likely, to crash.

The process relates to the intellectual and the emotional – the "who, what, where, why, and when." Understanding the buying process is just as important as understanding the property. You need to know **who** is involved, **what** comes next, **where** to turn with questions, **why** the transaction happens in its specific sequence, and **when** each deadline must be met.

The property is the tangible – the land, building, lease, demographics and the surrounding retail corridor. It is important for you to understand the various property choices, differences, advantages and disadvantages, and to put these attributes into an understandable context.

If you understand the property but don't understand the process, you will be out of balance. When you understand both, the entire transaction will make sense. You will be able to make confident and informed choices. You will ask intelligent questions, cross-check your attorney and your broker, and ensure you are prepared for the transition to ownership.

## When and How Do You Receive Rent?

Property owners love the first of the month because that's when rent is due. When the third day of the month comes and your tenant has not dropped off your rent check, you start to wonder. When the seventh day of the month passes and your check still has not arrived, you cringe. Thoughts of eviction and lawyers creep into your mind. Does this sound familiar?

These thoughts should disappear when you own a NNN property. If you chose a quality tenant and your property is well located, your rent should arrive like clockwork every month, every year, every decade. Rent will arrive by check or by direct deposit. Some tenants give you the choice of delivery; other tenants will mandate one method or the other. Whether the money arrives in your mailbox or is deposited directly into your bank account, a NNN property should be the easiest real estate investment you will ever own. It will even be easier than owning your home.

## Chapter 5: From Letter of Intent to Closing

## What Is a Letter of Intent?

A Letter of Intent (LOI) is a non-binding agreement between the buyer and seller. It is perhaps the least confusing form used in the purchase of a NNN property. It is short, one or two pages, and is usually prepared by your real estate broker. The LOI is intentionally kept simple. The forthcoming purchase contract will contain the formal legalese.

The LOI will outline the following items (sometimes more):

- Property address
- Purchase price
- Who is buying the property
- Amount of earnest money deposit
- Duration of contingency period
- Broker information
- Closing date
- Acceptance deadline

- Signature lines for buyer(s) and seller(s)

Once the buyer and seller agree to terms and finalize the LOI, a formal purchase contract is prepared (usually by the seller's attorney).

## Why an LOI Matters

In the old days, a deal was consummated by a handshake. A handshake was a promise between two people of honor. Today, in real estate terms, a handshake has been replaced by an LOI. An LOI is not quite as personal or binding as an old-fashioned handshake, but an honorable buyer and an honorable seller will follow through on the written promises they make to each other.

A seller has a moral obligation to sell the property to you and have his or her attorney write a purchase contract based on the terms of the signed LOI. If a better offer is received after signing an LOI, an honorable seller should decline the new offer.

You, as the buyer, have a moral obligation to purchase the property based on the LOI you signed. If you find another property that interests you, you should take a pass on the new property (unless you have the ability to purchase both).

The LOI and subsequent purchase contract will have a contingency period during which you can visit the property, review the lease and other due diligence items provided by the seller, and order a survey and an environmental report. Although canceling shouldn't be your intent, if the property does not meet your reasonable expectations, it is acceptable to cancel the purchase contract. Your broker should support your choice.

**Use the 96% Rule**

Have you heard of the 96% Rule? The rule says that if you are 96% sure about any property, it is the right property for you to purchase. When it comes to deciding when you should submit an LOI to purchase a property, use the 96% rule. This rule stops at 96%

because it is nearly impossible to be more than 96% sure about any property.

If you plan to purchase a NNN property within the next few months, now is the perfect time to "window shop." Ask your broker many questions and make sure you request and review many property brochures. This study period will help you understand the nuances of the NNN property market. It is very difficult to become 96% confident about a specific property until you understand the NNN property marketplace and are comfortable with the buying process.

## LOI Before You Fly

When you are 96% sure about a property, you should submit an LOI immediately. The second biggest mistake an indecisive buyer makes is to ponder, sleep on it, and over-analyze. The biggest mistake an indecisive buyer makes is to purchase an airline ticket or drive a long distance to view a property before securing the property with an LOI.

Here's a hypothetical story – A property with a strong tenant and great location just hit the market. You are 96% sure the property is right for you. You purchase an airline ticket, drive to the airport, fly to another state, rent a car, drive to the property, confirm you love the property, drive back to the airport, catch your return flight, drive home, call your real estate broker and submit an LOI. By the time your LOI is submitted, you find out the seller has received and accepted an LOI from another buyer. Unfortunately, this story has a happy ending for the other buyer, not for you.

Remember, buying real estate is all about controlling the property. If you are 96% confident about a property, seize the opportunity before your competition (another buyer) seizes it first. In other words, LOI before you fly.

**Timeline of Your Purchase**

Step 1: You submit an LOI to the seller. The seller signs and returns your LOI within one to three days.

Step 2: The seller has his or her attorney prepare a purchase contract. This usually takes between a few days and a week.

Step 3: Your attorney reviews the purchase contract and sends comments to the seller's attorney. This usually takes between a few days and a week.

Step 4: Your attorney and the seller's attorney negotiate contract terms and agree to a final contract. This usually takes between a few days and several weeks.

Step 5: Your due diligence period begins. The negotiated due diligence timeframe is usually between 14 and 30 days.

Step 6: You close on the property. Closing usually happens within 14 days from the completion of your due diligence period. Buyer and seller sign their respective documents and then FedEx them to the closing agent.

The timeline above is relatively standard, assuming the property is not under construction. Closing will take an additional 30-60 days if you need a loan.

## Do You Need an Attorney?

The simple answer is yes, you need an attorney.

Nobody likes paying an attorney. Even attorneys don't like paying other attorneys. However, the cost of paying a qualified real estate attorney to ensure all components of your purchase are correct is usually much less than paying an attorney to correct a problem after you have purchased the property.

Your attorney will review your purchase contract to ensure all proper representations, warranties, ownership entities, timelines and contingencies are in place. Your attorney will review the lease, tenant financials, loan documents (if applicable), title commitment, estoppel certificate, survey, Phase 1 Environmental Site Assessment, deed and other items during your due diligence period. Last but not least, your attorney will review a stack of closing documents.

## Should You Visit the Property?

You are able to drive up and down almost any street from your computer using Google Street View ® or www.showmystreet.com. A property brochure often will provide area demographics, property photos, and an aerial photo showing the surrounding retail tenants, hospitals, schools and residential subdivisions. A surveyor, environmental company, engineer and appraiser can detail the tangible aspects of the property.

Here's another multi-million-dollar question you should ask yourself: "Is this analysis sufficient?"

Some buyers conclude the above analysis is sufficient and never visit the property themselves. In addition, some buyers believe that if the location and building are good enough for the national tenant who signs the lease and occupies the property, it is good enough for them. Other buyers would never purchase a property without visiting it first.

**Why the Estoppel Certificate is Important**

A lease signed by a strong tenant should be bankable. But how do you, as the purchaser, know if there is conflict between the current property owner and the tenant? The concept "trust but verify" is achieved through the estoppel certificate. The estoppel certificate is a written representation from the tenant to the property owner. If there is a conflict, it will show up in the estoppel certificate. There will be no place for the seller to hide.

The estoppel certificate identifies the existing lease, all modifications and amendments. In addition, it confirms the lease is in full force and effect with no defaults, and there are no unfulfilled landlord obligations.

The estoppel certificate is an important part of your purchase. Your purchase contract and closing should be contingent upon receiving a current, signed and acceptable estoppel certificate from the tenant.

## Chapter 6:  1031 Exchange

### What Is a 1031 Exchange?

Here's what a 1031 exchange means to you in one simple sentence – You are able to sell investment property, purchase other investment property, and defer the applicable taxes.

More specifically, section 1031 of the Internal Revenue Code is a tool investors utilize when they sell investment property and reinvest all proceeds into new property of equal or greater value.  When you follow the specific rules, you are able to defer 100% of your Depreciation Recapture Tax, State Capital Gains Tax and Federal Capital Gains Tax.

Let's review the key terms:

Depreciation Recapture Tax – When you own an investment property, a percentage of the building and other improvements are depreciated each year.  Over time, year after year, the aggregate depreciation can add up to a significant amount of money. If you sell your investment property and do not utilize a 1031 exchange, you must repay the IRS a portion of the money previously depreciated.

State Capital Gains Tax – If you are a resident of a state that has a state capital gains tax and allows Like-Kind exchange deferral, and you do not utilize a 1031 exchange when you sell your investment property, you will be responsible for paying applicable State Capital Gains Tax where you legally reside.

Federal Capital Gains Tax – If you sell an investment property anywhere in the United States and you do not utilize a 1031 exchange, you will be responsible for paying applicable Federal Capital Gains Tax to the IRS.

Please make sure to consult with your CPA and attorney regarding state, federal, and IRC §1031 rules, requirements, suitability and compliance.

## What Is Like-Kind Property?

Like-Kind Property, with respect to real estate, is a term that describes nearly any investment property that is not used as your primary or personal residence, or for other personal use. You are able to 1031 exchange nearly any Like-Kind real estate for any other Like-Kind real estate.

Like-Kind is one of the many rules of 1031 exchange. The term Like-Kind sounds very specific. However, the scope of Like-Kind is very broad. All of the following real estate qualifies as Like-Kind: land, office building (even if you work there), rental house, rental condo, apartment building, shopping center, industrial property, mixed use property and NNN property.

For example, you are able to 1031 exchange vacant land for an apartment building, an office building for a shopping center, rental house for vacant land, any of these or other Like-Kind real estate for a NNN property.

## Should You 1031 or Pay the Taxes?

Very few people like paying taxes. If your property has enjoyed significant appreciation, unfortunately you will have a significant tax bill if you sell your property and don't utilize a 1031 exchange.

Perhaps the question above is best answered mathematically. If you pay Recapture Tax + State Capital Gains Tax + Federal Capital Gains Tax, how much money will you pay to the government and how much money will remain for you? If your tax bill is small, you may opt to pay the taxes. If your tax bill is large, a 1031 exchange is almost always the better choice.

For easy math, let's use the example of selling a property for $4,000,000 with a $1,000,000 tax obligation if you don't utilize a 1031 exchange. Compare the income you will receive from doing a 1031 exchange into a NNN property with a 6% annual return versus the income you will receive from an alternative investment that also has a 6% annual return.

The NNN property will yield $240,000 ($4,000,000 x 6%). The alternative investment will only yield $180,000 ($3,000,000 x 6%).

## Four Reasons Why Investors Utilize 1031 Exchange

Reason #1 is to defer both Capital Gains and Depreciation Recapture Tax. See above if you skipped that section.

Reason #2 is to consolidate. Whether you own rental houses, apartment buildings, shopping centers or any other combination of investment properties, consolidating may make your life easier. For example, you are able to sell multiple properties and 1031 exchange into fewer properties.

Reason #3 is to diversify. If all of your properties are in one asset class (residential, commercial, etc.), you can diversify your portfolio by selling some of the properties and 1031 exchanging into another asset class. In addition, if all of your properties are located in one geographic area, you can diversify into other locations.

Reason #4 is to simplify your life. If you own management-intensive property, you can 1031 exchange into NNN property and leave all maintenance and repairs to your tenant.

## Who Holds Your Money?

There is a period of time between when you sell a property and purchase a new one. During this transitional timeframe, you are not able to touch (also known as having actual or constructive receipt) your 1031 exchange proceeds. Your money should be safeguarded by a 1031 exchange Qualified Intermediary. Your Qualified Intermediary will hold your money (preferably in a segregated account under a Qualified Escrow or Trust Agreement in a depository institution), prepare the exchange documents and guide you through the entire exchange process.

Your Qualified Intermediary must be a disinterested third party. Your attorney, CPA, real estate broker, etc. are not able to act as your Qualified Intermediary. It is important for your Qualified Intermediary to have sufficient experience, insurance, fidelity bond, secure banking and other safeguards in place to ensure your 1031 exchange proceeds are protected.

## Timeframe & Identification Rules

There are two concurrent timeframes (rules) that you must follow when doing a 1031 exchange. The first timeframe (45 days) relates to property identification. The second timeframe (180 days) specifies the latest date on which you are allowed to close the property or properties you have identified.

The 45-day identification period begins the day after you close your property sale (relinquished property). Before the end of day 45, you must submit a written identification form to your Qualified Intermediary. The identification form (provided by your Qualified Intermediary) will specify the price and address of the property or properties you intend to purchase or have targeted as a backup in case your primary property does not close.

The IRS limits the amount of property you are allowed to identify (more rules). The two most common rules for identification are the **Three Property Rule** and the **200% Rule**. The Three Property Rule allows you to identify up to three properties, regardless of the aggregate price. The 200% Rule allows you to identify an unlimited number of properties, as long as the total value of all of the identified properties does not exceed 200% of the value of the property you sold. For example, under the 200% rule, if you sold a property for $2,000,000, you can identify as many properties as you like as long as the total value does not exceed $4,000,000.

Similar to the 45-day identification period, the 180-day period also begins the day after you close your property sale. From this first day, you have up to 180 days to close any and all replacement property that will be included in your 1031 exchange. Please note that

180 is the maximum number of days. You are allowed to close your relinquished property and your replacement property on the same day or any day up to day 180.

There is one caveat to the 180-day rule. The latest date on which you are allowed to close your replacement property is whichever comes first – 180 days after you close your relinquished property OR when you file your tax return. Therefore, if you closed your relinquished property in December and you have not completed your 1031 exchange by your tax filing deadline, make sure you file an extension for your tax return. Once you file your tax return for the previous year, your 1031 exchange deadline automatically ends.

## Purchasing Your Replacement Property

Purchasing replacement property is the enjoyable and rewarding part of your 1031 exchange. You will transition from property that did not coincide with your long-term plans to replacement property that will be a better long-term fit.

Your CPA and 1031 exchange Qualified Intermediary can calculate to the penny how much money your replacement property must be in order to have maximum tax deferral.

For simplicity, here are two general rules to follow:

Rule #1: You must reinvest the entire net equity (cash proceeds) from your sale into replacement property.

Rule #2: Your replacement property must be equal or greater in value to the property you sold (minus broker fees, title insurance and other standard closing costs).

Here are a few examples:

#1: You sell property for $2,000,000 (with no loan) and have $100,000 in closing costs. Your replacement property must be at least $1,900,000. You must reinvest your $1,900,000 equity into the new property.

#2: You sell property for $2,000,000 (with a $1,000,000 loan) and have $100,000 in closing costs.

Your replacement property must be at least $1,900,000. You must reinvest your $900,000 equity and obtain a new loan for $1,000,000.

#3: You sell property for $2,000,000 (with a $500,000 loan) and have $100,000 in closing costs. Your replacement property must be at least $1,900,000. You must reinvest your $1,400,000 equity and obtain a new loan for $500,000.

Here are two more rules: First – If financially able, you are allowed to offset all or part of your existing loan with additional cash (if your goal is to have less debt or be debt-free). Second – If your replacement property is a higher price than your sale property, the difference can come from either additional cash or an additional loan.

## How Should You Take Title?

Your upfront choices will have a direct impact on your future 1031 exchange options. Here are a few thoughts about ownership entities and how you should take title.

An attorney or CPA will usually recommend that a client purchase investment property in a Limited Liability Company (LLC), not individually. Trusts and other structures exist but an LLC is the most common ownership entity. If you purchase an investment property with a friend(s) or relative(s), it may be advisable for each investor to have his or her own LLC and to take title as Tenants-in-Common.

When an investment property is sold by one LLC, that entity usually will be the purchaser of the 1031 exchange replacement property or properties. If there is more than one owner of the LLC, all owners must purchase the replacement property or properties together; the LLC owners are not able to purchase property separately. This could be problematic (see story below.)

When an investment property is sold by more than one LLC (and title is held as Tenants-in-Common), each LLC will complete its own separate 1031 exchange. This means each LLC owner can 1031 exchange into property together or they can separate and purchase any other property they choose.

Quick story – 1031tax.com has helped countless family members and business partners purchase NNN property through a 1031 exchange. Some would never purchase property without their partner; others no longer speak with their partner. When business partners want a "divorce" and own property in one LLC, it is very messy, not to mention taxing, if they do not do a 1031 exchange. The moral of this story is before you purchase property, make sure you discuss with your attorney and CPA the ownership entities and how you will take title. This upfront cost will be money well spent.

# 1031 Exchange Until You Die

Most people have heard the saying, "Nothing is certain except for death and taxes." 1031 exchange is the exception.

When investment property that has appreciated in value is sold, there will be a tax liability. However, if you or your children inherit investment property, the property will have a stepped-up basis. Stepped-up basis means the property value is readjusted to the current market value, not the price the property was purchased for. Depending on the value of the estate, you or your children may not have any tax liability when property in inherited.

## Chapter 7:  Why Work With 1031tax.com

## The 1031tax.com Team

Four people anchor 1031tax.com.  Here are their profiles:

Alan Fruitman is a family man with a wife, daughter and son.  Alan is the author of this book and a recognized expert in NNN property.  He has been interviewed by, and written articles for, many regional and national publications.  He is the founder of 1031tax.com and the President & Managing Broker of Real Estate Foundation, Inc.  Alan began selling real estate in 1993, during his final semester at Colorado State University, where he earned a degree in economics.

Alan's first real estate sale was a residential house bought by the manager of the restaurant where Alan worked part-time.  During seven years of residential sales, Alan sold more than 300 properties.  In the beginning of his career, Alan was young and not yet established in his community. He needed to find a niche that separated him from the thousands of other real estate brokers. Alan discovered, through public records searches, the names and addresses of property owners who lived in other states. Before long, he specialized in selling rental houses and helping his clients utilize 1031 exchanges. One day, a client asked about exchanging his rental houses for a NNN property. That's when everything changed.

The transition out of residential property happened fast. Alan created 1031tax.com when the Internet was in its relative infancy. When 1031tax.com went online, leads poured in (There was limited competition back then). Fast forward to 2014. Alan has helped several hundred NNN property buyers purchase more than a billion dollars worth of NNN property.

Elizabeth Laesecke is the Vice President of Real Estate Foundation, Inc. and a licensed real estate broker. Elizabeth has been an anchor of the 1031tax.com team since 2005. Elizabeth is married and has two daughters and four grandsons. She has worked in the real estate industry since 1969 and has experience in development, operations, community planning and brokerage.

Jim Slinkard is an independent real estate broker who works with 1031tax.com. Jim has been in the real estate industry since 1974. He has sold thousands of properties and managed thousands of real estate brokers. In fact, Jim hired Alan to work in his Keller Williams Realty office in 1993. Jim has one son and twin granddaughters.

Pamela Keith is an analyst at Real Estate Foundation, Inc. Pamela helps review and send NNN properties to our buyers every day. Pamela has four children.

**Broker Relationships**

While most real estate brokers focus on representing sellers, 1031tax.com focuses on buyers. This means 1031tax.com is not a competitor to listing brokers. In fact, listing brokers love 1031tax.com because its buyers purchase their listings. 1031tax.com has cultivated tremendous relationships with other real estate brokers. These relationships and a track record of successful closings are the reason brokers frequently send 1031tax.com their new listings before they are marketed to the general public.

**What Buyers Need to Hear**

New clients of 1031tax.com are surprised when we tell them "no". Because we listen to our clients' perspective, learn about their long-term goals, pay attention to their risk tolerance and understand what is important to them, it is easy to suggest that a client not purchase certain properties. It is not that we don't want our clients to purchase property; rather it is that we don't want our clients to purchase the wrong property.

Clients also hear "yes" from 1031tax.com. YES – We will share our opinions, support you if you decline a property, identify properties you may have overlooked and tell you what you need to hear, not what you want to hear.

The purchase transaction is temporary. A relationship is permanent. When clients know they are valued more than a commission, their real estate broker becomes an irreplaceable advocate and friend.

**Most Clients Are Referred**

Real estate brokers at 1031tax.com are blessed with tremendous relationships. We spend our time building and cultivating relationships, preparing for and being present when we speak with our clients.

Past clients, attorneys, CPAs and other real estate brokers are the source of most of our business. Past clients want their friends to experience the same personalized service and to acquire quality NNN properties as they have. Attorneys, CPAs and other real estate brokers frequently refer their clients for the same reasons.

## You Will Be Prepared for Success

Because the market for NNN property is ultra-competitive, 1031tax.com is **ready, willing and able** to prepare you for success.

Ready means 1031tax.com will help you understand the process and the properties, help you define your investment criteria, answer all your questions, and send new NNN properties to you almost every Monday, Tuesday, Wednesday, Thursday and Friday. Properties will be off-market, pre-market and first day on the market.

Willing means 1031tax.com will allocate time and resources to work closely with you, your attorney and your CPA.

Able means 1031tax.com has the relationships and proven track record to diligently guide you throughout your NNN property purchase…and beyond.

## References Matter

The following are references from past clients, attorneys, CPA's and other real estate brokers:

---

Finally, a book that helps explain how this all works in plain English! Alan's book is accessible by anyone - including recovering lawyers like myself - and that's saying something.

I'd recommend this for anyone interested in learning more about buying NNN property.

\-     Patrick S. Ryan, J.D., Ph.D.
Strategy & Operations Principal at Google Inc.

At first I was a bit skeptical, purchasing brick and mortar real estate from a firm that refers to itself as 1031tax.com, but Alan proved his vast knowledge and professionalism of 1031 properties right out of the gate. I was not new to real estate, but had to get up to speed fast on 1031 NNN properties as our downleg transaction was moving along fast. We've succeeded in diversifying our portfolio to include the purchase of properties with several high quality tenants such as McDonald's, O'Reilly Auto Parts, 7-Eleven, Chipotle and Panera Bread. All of the locations are in prime retail areas that we feel will meet the test of time.

Alan had the time and patience to get me up to speed quickly and helped me develop a timeline to work within. He's always been available and willing to help out at any time with whatever issues arise during the course of my transactions. I'm nearly halfway through with my exchanges and am very satisfied with the quality of the NNN properties we've acquired so far. Alan is my "go to" guy.

- Michael Solondz

I have worked with Alan Fruitman for more than 15 years and have referred several of my clients to him for real estate services in addition to purchasing several properties of my own. Alan's attention to detail, knowledge, and professionalism are the reasons for his longevity and success in the real estate business. It is with the utmost confidence I will continue to refer my clients to Alan.

- Todd K. Schiff, CPA

---

I am grateful to know and have Alan Fruitman represent our family's investments in commercial real estate. His wisdom and advice in this area are un-matched. Rather than being driven for the closing so he would be paid, I found Alan intense to represent me well. His thorough analysis is unmatched. He is passionate about representing his client and the best interests of his client. This book is just another example of his desire to educate his clients.

- Steve Booren

When the time came to initiate a 1031 exchange purchase, we contacted Alan Fruitman because he had been staying in contact with us for two years via email notices. He was very helpful in guiding us through the exchange purchase process in a very professional and friendly manner. He facilitated all communications with the seller and provided all necessary paperwork in connection with the purchase, making the experience much easier.

During the whole process, from beginning to end, Alan would always follow up with phone calls that made us feel he really had our best interests at heart.

We felt very comfortable working with Alan and highly recommend his services to any client. We owned a NNN property before and liked the idea of receiving passive income with no landlord responsibility so Alan was our best choice in helping us find another NNN property to suit our needs.

- Ross and Linda Greco

One of the things I appreciate the most about owning NNN properties is that it keeps my income stream consistent. For years I owned small apartment buildings and I made good money doing it, but I was constantly at the mercy of changing market conditions. If the insurance industry got nervous about something, my rates would fluctuate dramatically almost overnight. If the local taxing authority assessed my property for too much, I was forced to spend time and money contesting their value and usually did not win. But, with my NNN properties, I no longer have to worry about those issues.

There are two things that separate Alan Fruitman from all the other people that I have dealt with in the real estate industry. The first is that he is almost always immediately available for me when I pick up the phone to call him. No messages, no call backs, no appointments necessary. The second is that he has established an extensive network of quality professionals in almost every state of the country. No matter where I search for and find a property, he is able to connect me with reliable professionals to help me close on my property without any problems.

Alan listens and learns about his clients. He finds out what his clients are really looking for and what they really need. Then he helps them work through all the options to find the best match possible. He doesn't sell them on the easiest or best thing for himself. I truly believe he would rather sell nothing than lead his clients to a deal that was not good for them.

- Vance Hunt

---

From start to finish Alan was swift, attentive, receptive and extremely informative. His wisdom, database and market knowledge guided us intuitively to secure a $15M commercial Trophy Property. One of Alan's finest qualities was how calm, confident and reassuring he was during the intense negotiation process. I will continue to work with and refer Alan to anyone involved in a 1031 exchange.

- Kara Fiore

We have worked with Alan Fruitman since 1999. Alan has assisted us in converting our equity interests in management-intensive shopping centers into management-free net leases while avoiding tax recognition through Section 1031 exchanges. Alan and his colleagues at his company 1031tax.com have been instrumental in our acquisition of properties leased to, among other leading tenants, Walgreens, CVS, McDonald's, Burger King, Chili's, Rite Aid, AutoZone, etc.

The newsletter published by 1031tax.com keeps us informed about current developments in the Section 1031 marketplace. We can count on Alan not only to identify transactions of potential interest to us but to work with us diligently toward a successful closing. We have recommended Alan's services to many associates in the real estate industry.

We expect to continue to avail ourselves of the expertise of Alan and the 1031tax.com team in the future.

-    Marilyn Joy and Walter Samuels

I have been in commercial real estate for 40 years. I first met Alan Fruitman in 2003 through an associate of mine.

During the last 11 years, Alan and I have collaborated on over $70 million worth of 1031 exchange properties.

Alan is one of the most competent real estate professionals I have ever met during my career and his integrity, honor and dignity as a person and professional are beyond reproach.

Of all the transactions in which we have been involved, not one required a written agreement between us as all was done on our word and handshake.

In short, Alan's word is his bond—what greater compliment can there be to a person or professional?

- Michael J. Antonoplos

I have years of experience in building and operating single family and multifamily residential pieces, as well as commercial retail and office parcels. But I had little experience in free standing credit tenant investing prior to meeting Alan. Alan continues to provide me with the education of his meaningful experience, opening me up to opportunities of trading some of our assets into properties credit tenanted on free standing parcels.

We are in the process of acquiring a credit tenanted free-standing parcel at the moment, without a trade (as the absence of a trade does not interfere with the value to us of this piece). Alan is careful to be responsive without being directive, while at the same time seeking to make certain that I avoid tripping and hurting myself.

He has been a pleasure to work with over the last few years, and I look forward to continuing to work with him for many years into the future.

- Arnie Malk

Alan Fruitman is the most knowledgeable commercial real estate agent regarding NNN Properties that I have met. I purchased my 4th NNN property from Alan and it went so easy.

One thing I really like is that when I need information about different properties, Alan gets right on it and I have an answer within 1 day. Alan has given me advice about the latest properties on the market.

I started my first NNN property in 1981 and it was the best thing I ever did. Owning NNN property is so easy, very little work is needed and it seems to me much safer than the stock market. You have less risk and guaranteed return with less exposure.

I really enjoy talking to Alan because of his knowledge which really helps me follow the properties for sale.

-   Bob Schoenbachler

Working with Alan Fruitman was an excellent experience. When we started to sell some property that had been in the family for several generations, we were not familiar with the 1031 process.

Alan was a tremendous resource and his experience was invaluable. Choosing a 1031 property can be financially rewarding, but one must be extremely careful to choose the right property.

I cannot emphasize how important it is to work with a broker who is knowledgeable about the 1031 process, who can find the "right" property to fit your financial requirements and who will steer you away from the numerous potential pitfalls that you will encounter during the exchange process.

For our family, Alan was the perfect broker. I probably receive ten calls a month from other 1031 brokers. I would not use anyone other than Alan.

-   Rich F.

I feel completely confident working with Alan on identifying triple-net properties that are consistent with our investment strategy.

We frequently communicate and I get daily listings on properties that are tailored to our needs. Alan has provided guidance as it relates to the individual properties and the best investment at any given time. His relationships with other brokers and his credibility and integrity are verified through my various discussions with numerous real estate professionals.

We have purchased over ten triple-net properties through Alan and I've been able to learn, not only how to analyze the assets, but also to get a better feel for real estate throughout the country.

I unequivocally recommend Alan based on his professionalism and level of diligence that have effectuated the numerous transactions on which we have worked.

- Julio Peterson

We needed to find three replacement properties for my in-laws to complete a 1031 exchange under an extremely tight timeframe. Having been involved in over $15 billion of real estate acquisitions over the past 20 years, I didn't think I needed a lot of guidance.

However, after a large NYC real estate hedge fund referred me to Alan, it became apparent that buying NNN was unlike purchasing multi-tenant properties. From that point on, I stopped working with, and looking at offerings from other brokers and worked exclusively with Alan. Alan provided much needed guidance and information necessary for us to choose the right properties to match our credit risk and investment horizon. He communicated issues and concerns well and kept the process moving at a quick pace.

Without any reservation I would recommend Alan to anyone who is looking to purchase NNN property in any part of the country.

- Rob Friedberg

Working with Alan Fruitman is a real pleasure.

Alan not only demonstrated competency in real estate investing, but he also demonstrated integrity by putting my interest first. Alan even counseled me to skip a questionable offering even when I had submitted an LOI through him. He said to the effect that "Let's wait for something better." We had never worked together before that, but he already committed my interest above his.

Alan never pushed me to consummate any deal for his benefit but gave me room to consider my own circumstances. In my subsequent deal with him, he counseled me to stay on a deal when my buyer remorse kicked in. Indeed, in hindsight, it was a deal not to be missed, and I am glad I listened to Alan.

I am glad Alan was in that deal with me.

- Alex T. Kwei

A friend introduced me to Alan Fruitman in 2008. I was selling a multi-tenant property in Brooklyn and wanted to 1031 exchange into a single tenant NNN property. Alan and his team patiently shared insightful information and helped me buy a NNN property in a world-class location. I am now in the process of buying another NNN property and value the nationwide inventory of new properties Alan sends to me every day.

In addition, I confidently refer my friends to 1031tax.com.

- Anthony Conte

---

Alan is a true expert in NNN properties. His years of experience, his broad network and his deep expertise combine to enable his clients to obtain the optimal properties that fit their investment goals.

- Jeff Tucker

As I entered the NNN property market, I got a coach and a mentor in addition to a broker. Alan provided the guidance I needed to better understand NNN properties and has always been a great source of information.

My success is, in no small way, due to the commitment Alan and his staff made to me.

- David Roussos

---

If one is interested in navigating the labyrinth known as Internal Revenue Code 1031 Tax Free Real Estate Exchanges, please contact Alan Fruitman. The many nuances of the tax code are complex and potentially a financial "Titanic."

Contact Alan. He is a knowledgeable and experienced professional.

- David K.

Working with Alan has been an enlightening experience. He is very well versed in our craft and I have learned some new aspects of our industry from him.

Alan pointed out the importance of the percentage of rent to the gross sales of the store. He can analyze a deal as well as anyone I have ever met. Through Alan I am enjoying a steady stream of rental income during my retirement.

I strongly recommend that anyone interested in single tenant net leases speak to Alan first.

Even if you don't buy anything it's a good learning experience just talking to him.

- Marty Novick

My wife Linda and I have been investing in residential real estate since 1975. After managing rental properties for most of our lives we wanted to simplify our lives and real estate holdings and decided to purchase a NNN property.

Alan Fruitman and his team at 1031tax.com helped us purchase our first NNN property in 2011. Alan knew we were unfamiliar with this style of ownership and walked us through the process. They could not have made us any more comfortable in our acquisition through their team effort.

In 2013, Alan helped us purchase a second NNN property. We trust Alan and his team 100% and have confidently referred several of our friends to him.

Alan's character, communication skills and knowledge of NNN property is unparalleled.

- Murray and Linda Acheson

Alan Fruitman and his team at 1031tax.com have been an important contributor to the successful strategic approach of our firm in the commercial real estate space.

We encountered Alan over a decade ago and have done business with and consulted with him ever since.

Alan has always been willing to work with us, providing investment advice and properties to consider, whether it is on the buy or the sell side.

Alan and his team have the highest integrity and always stand ready to help. I highly endorse Alan and the 1031tax.com team's skills.

- Paul Olson

Working with Alan Fruitman was both pleasant and financially beneficial. His ability to help identify and invest in NNN properties made it simple to take advantage of the cumbersome IRS 1031 Exchange requirements.

My first venture into the world of NNN leases still provides a solid income 10 years later.

- Saul Tawil

---

I have been involved in over a thousand transactions and have dealt with numerous financial advisors.

Alan is very knowledgeable, methodical and operates with high integrity.

He is at the top of my list and I consider him the best in his field.

- Brandon Haddon
President OmniCredit

We were fortunate to find Alan Fruitman and 1031tax.com when we were looking for a 1031 exchange property.

Alan helped us locate and identify a Walgreens property that fit our demographic and yield criteria.

We were very happy with the guidance received from Alan and his team, and we were able to successfully close the transaction and still own the property to this day. We would not hesitate to contact Alan again with our 1031 or single tenant property needs.

- Suraj Sani

---

Thank you for all your help in making my recent acquisition. We looked at a lot of properties. Your advice was highly valued during the process, enabling me to select my property with great confidence.

You were a great mentor.

- Todd Myers

Alan has been very helpful with the acquisitions of triple net properties for our real estate portfolio.

Along with Alan's knowledge is his ability to communicate and educate, which proves extremely beneficial in creating a bond of trust.

Through many conversations we were able to identify and purchase properties which suit our many needs. NNN properties now make up 65% of our real estate holdings.

Managing multiple triple net properties is proving to be cost effective compared to multifamily and office retail.

For our needs and desires, NNN properties have proven to be a lucrative fit to our real estate portfolio.

- Howie Raymond

I contacted Alan on behalf of a client with respect to a target property to be purchased for retirement income (this was not a 1031 transaction) as a proxy for a part of the client's fixed income allocation.

Alan was extremely helpful and responsive throughout the process. He followed up with the seller's broker and the developer to assure all of our questions were answered promptly and he was proactive in raising issues we should consider addressing.

Our client had a cost segregation prepared to maximize the depreciation deductions, including bonus depreciation which generated a large first year tax loss. The loss was fully deductible as a result of a large passive capital gain recognized in the same tax year – a very positive result as the client had a long-term capital gain and an offsetting ordinary loss.

- Carl A Loden, CPA/PFS
Partner, Keiter

I have successfully closed two single tenant retail transactions with Alan Fruitman and found him to be both easy to work with and a consummate professional. Alan demonstrated excellent client communication throughout each step of the process in addition to superior market knowledge.

I would highly recommend his services and would welcome the opportunity to work with him again.

- Don McMinn
Marcus & Millichap

---

I have worked with Alan Fruitman for over a decade and have closed multiple transactions with his group. Alan provides constant communication with detailed information making the vetting process easier for us and our clients. I look forward to working with Alan and his team in the future.

- Will Pike
CBRE

Alan Fruitman makes me look like a genius to my clients. Many clients face a problem later in life. They are tired of the numerous hassles which arise from being a landlord. Yet, because of years of depreciation, they cannot sell their leasehold property without significant federal income tax consequences.

The answer to this problem comes through Alan. He finds a solid triple-net lease with a significant return, which return will continue to grow over the years. This allows my clients to sell their present property or properties and, through a 1031 Tax Free Exchange, roll those funds into a hassle free investment, which will give them a monthly stream of income for years to come.

Alan is great to work with, always available, and ready with clear, unbiased advice. In the end, because of Alan's hard work, my clients think I'm a genius. Thank you, Alan!

- William S. Dick, Esq.
Dick, Stein, Schemel, Wine & Frey, LLP

Thank you for your assistance in the purchase, 4.5 years ago, of my NN property in Florida.

The process of reviewing, choosing and negotiating properties with your assistance was very simple. I knew I had an advocate during the entire process. Although I am aware there is risk and NN or NNN properties may not be for everyone, I have surely appreciated having this property as a portion of my portfolio.

I know from receiving many inquiries and offers that there are many, many "brokers" out there offering various NN/NNN properties. I would recommend anyone considering such an investment to consider Alan as their representative as he answered my questions, did what he said he would do and followed-up on matters as a professional.

Thanks Alan for your help with my purchase and let's continue to keep in touch.

- Van Jones

Many of us in our company have worked with Alan Fruitman for several years. One of our lines of business is to provide IRC section 1031 Qualified Intermediary and Like-Kind exchange services, and our clients often request a referral to providers of replacement properties.

I feel completely comfortable referring our clients to Alan, as I know that they will receive current market information with sufficient variety to suit their specific needs. Alan is very professional and knowledgeable. He is well aware of the opportunities in the marketplace, and which opportunities serve the needs of specific clients.

I have mutual clients with Alan who have achieved a positive outcome and have returned to Alan for more opportunities. I plan to continue to refer our clients who are seeking 1031 replacement properties to Alan Fruitman.

- William P. Lopriore, Jr.
  NES Financial

I had the good fortune of meeting Alan Fruitman approximately 10 years ago when doing research about 1031 Tax Exchanges. At that time I was in need of a rather large tax exchange property for a close friend of mine.

Alan exhibited the patience of a true champion. That is, his devotion to the project went far beyond the fee he would ultimately enjoy. He painstakingly navigated the process for this buyer, who was somewhat unfamiliar with the 1031 Exchange process, in a way that provided the buyer with absolute certainty about his eventual decision.

From one cold call to 10 years later, while my needs have varied, I know with confidence, that if I put Alan on the case, something positive will result from it. The only tough part I had with Alan was the fact that the Internet service I was working with at the time was in dial up mode.

- Eliot Tawil
Wharton Properties

Alan and I became friends and business acquaintances in 2005, when he sold one of my listings. Since then, we have maintained our friendship and have meaningful discussions about market conditions, cap rates, and college football.

Alan and I make it a point to meet every year at the ICSC real estate convention in Las Vegas. While there are many things I like about Alan and the people at 1031tax.com, the main thing I like is the way they do business.

I send all of my listings to Alan because he has a tremendous pool of buyers and does not compete with other brokers for listings.

I highly recommend Alan Fruitman and 1031tax.com to any NNN property buyer and to any broker who has NNN property for sale.

- Bob Manor
Coldwell Banker Commercial AI Group

It has been a pleasure to work with Alan Fruitman over the years.

It can be difficult to find honest and knowledgeable brokers in the net lease market today, but I can say that Alan is one of the few that really knows his stuff and has his client's best interest in mind. He is very professional and always very responsive and efficient.

My experience working with Alan has definitely been a positive one and I look forward to working with him again on future transactions.

- Derrick Schroeder
Solid Investments of Berger Realty Group

Alan Fruitman and his team at 1031tax.com are one of the only NNN property brokers I trust to work with my clients. Since I exclusively focus on arranging financing for NNN property, Alan and 1031tax.com are the perfect strategic partners for my company and my clients looking to purchase NNN property such as Walgreens, CVS, Advance Auto Parts,  Dollar General, Chase Bank and many others.

I am 100% comfortable and confident in referring my clients to Alan Fruitman and his team.  They have a tremendous amount of knowledge and experience in representing NNN property buyers and in the intricacies of 1031 exchange.

Alan and his team are also involved in the International Council of Shopping Centers, where they work with many developers and network with other real estate brokers to find "off market" NNN properties.

I have arranged acquisition financing for several of Alan's buyers and the experience was tremendously positive. I most recently arranged financing for one of Alan's clients' who purchased a flagship corporate Walgreens, O'Reilly Auto Parts and Dollar General.

I look forward to working with Alan, his team and his clients / associates that need financing for NNN property.

Alan and his organization are very professional, ethical and trustworthy, and I believe the core values of our companies are very much aligned.

I look forward to continuing my strategic alliance with 1031tax.com and assisting their clients.

\-   Christian S. Marabella<br>
Marabella Commercial Finance, Inc.

Many of my clients find that their tax situation is driving them to do a 1031 exchange. In some cases they are tired of the headaches of "tenants and toilets".

Alan Fruitman and his company, 1031tax.com, offer the replacement property solutions that my clients need plus the control of owning property without having to deal with other partners.

Alan has always been efficient and professional when working with my clients.

- Chris Sayre
Your Castle Real Estate

# Notes

# Notes

Made in the USA
Lexington, KY
04 February 2017